THE ADVENTURES OF
BRAVO and BUSTER
AT NEW SMYRNA BEACH

Written by: Elizabeth Martinell

Illustrated by: Roka Studio

About the Author:

Elizabeth **"Beth"** Martinell, is an energetic artist whose life blends creativity, spirituality, and a deep love for family. From her roots in New Jersey, to her current home in New Smyrna Beach, Florida, Beth's journey has been marked by resilience and passion. After a career in bartending and the medical field, she now channels her artistic talents into oil painting, furniture refurbishing, and various crafts. Beth is a proud mother of two sons, Joseph and Matthew, and a first-time grandparent to Joseph Felice Martinell. She shares her life with her fiancé Joe, two beloved dogs, Bravo and Buster, and a cherished cat named Obie.

Dedicated to:

Our loyal canine companions, Bravo and Buster, who came into our lives when we needed them the most and filled our lives with unconditional love, loyalty, and endless adventures. You remind us to embrace life's simple pleasures and cherish the beauty of each moment. Your presence makes the world a happier and more pleasant place. And to all the dogs who wag their tails and warm our hearts, this tale is for you.

A heartfelt acknowledgment to all the dreamers and believers who refuse to settle for mediocrity and strive to make a difference in the world, never settling for the ordinary. The beautiful coastline of New Smyrna Beach, where sun-drenched sands meet sky-blue waters, are forever etched in the hearts of our beach paradise, making dreams come true.

On a sunny afternoon in the quaint beach town of New Smyrna Beach, two playful dogs, Bravo and Buster, saw their chance for fun when their owners forgot to close the gate.

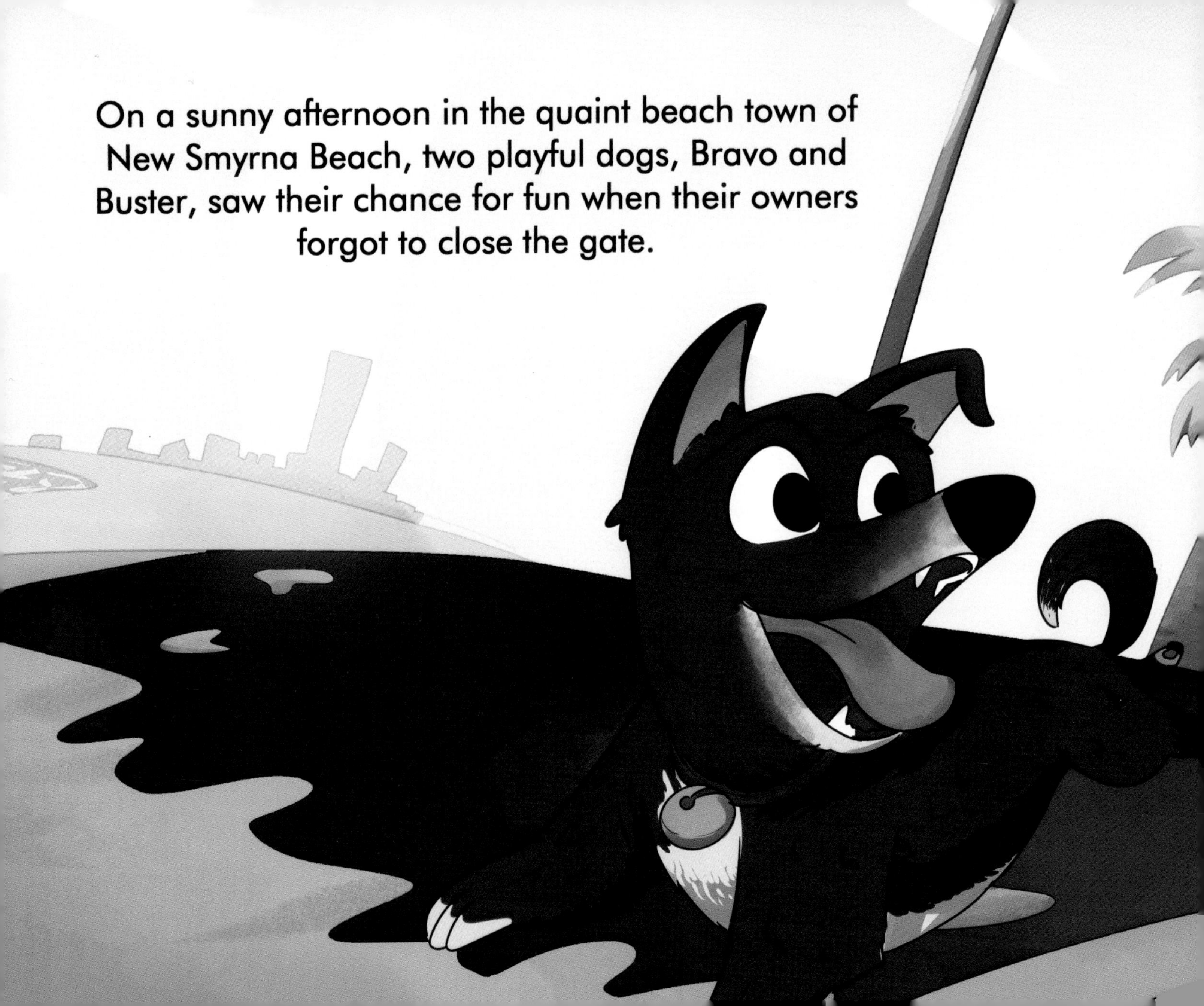

Bravo, with his shiny black fur, and Buster, with his fluffy brown coat, were the best of buddies. With excitement bubbling inside them and tails wagging, the two curious pups dashed down Flagler Avenue, their paws hitting the pavement as they headed for a beachside adventure.

Bravo and Buster got to the beach and saw cool white sand that looked like snow. Their tails wagging happily, they felt free as a bird and ran along the edge of the water with their paws making big splashes. They were having so much fun, feeling the warm sun on their backs.

As the two furry friends, Bravo and Buster, ran down the beach, they saw the big yellow lifeguard tower standing tall in the morning sky. It was early, so the lifeguards weren't there yet.

With sandy paws and happy barks, they ran around, played in the sand, and splashed in the water.

Bravo and Buster spotted a crab burying itself in a sandy hideout.

The two nosy dogs started digging to only find the crab got away and they got sand up their nose.

Buster's nose wiggles as he smells something funny in the air. With Bravo right behind him, they follow the strange smell and weird tracks to a spot in the sand. And guess what they find? A big turtle slowly heading back to the water.

Bravo and Buster stood back because the turtle was much larger than them. When it reaches the water, the two furry friends barked goodbye.

Off they went to explore more of the beach, noses to the ground and tails wagging like flags. Bravo and Buster zigzagged through the sand, finding all kinds of shells in different shapes and sizes.

They bent down to look closely at the shells and giggled with delight on the bright, sandy beach.

With tails wagging once again, Bravo and Buster dashed along the sandy beach, feeling the squishy sand beneath their paws. They played tag with seagulls, dug silly holes, and even tried to catch the foamy waves. They were having the time of their lives!

But, oh no! Just a little farther out in the water, they saw something mysterious swimming. It was a shark! New Smyrna Beach is known as the "Shark Bite Capital of the World." They ran away from the water as fast as their little legs could take them, knowing they were never in any danger at all.

As Bravo and Buster ran along the shore, they saw surfers riding the waves. Some surfers slid smoothly on the water, while others waited on their boards for the perfect wave.

Bravo and Buster barked happily and wagged their tails as if they were clapping. They knew New Smyrna Beach is famous for its great surfing.

Tired from their adventure, the two brave pups found a comfy spot on the beach and watched the birds. They saw sandpipers chirping in a group, a tall heron peeking from the dunes, and pelicans diving into the water, showing off their cool fishing moves.

Bravo and Buster were thirsty and covered in sand from head to tail. They decided it was time to go home.

As they walked along the beach, still excited from their adventure, Bravo heard a soft splashing noise. He barked happily, and Buster looked too. To their surprise, they saw dolphins playing just beyond the waves, swimming through the water.

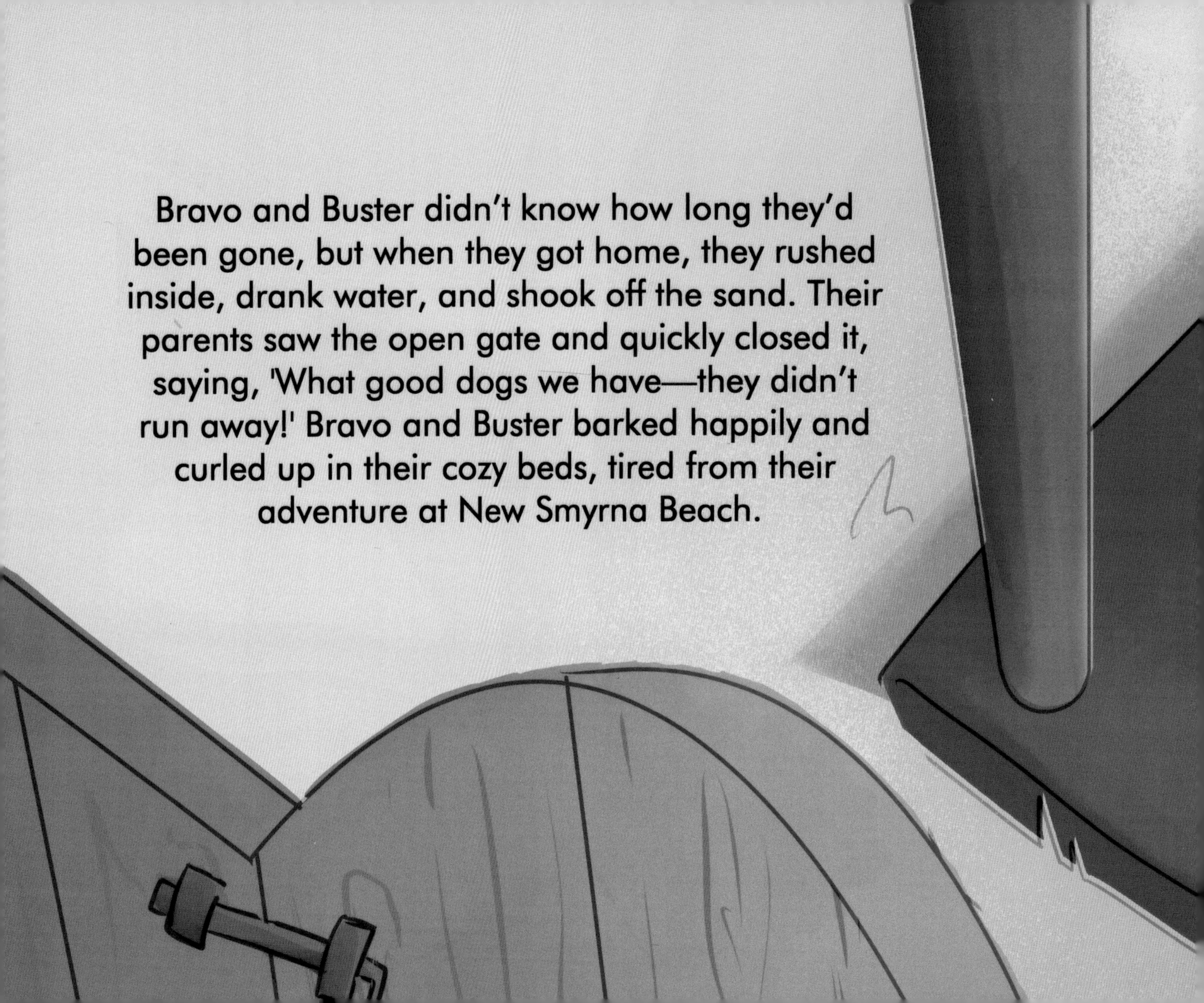

Bravo and Buster didn’t know how long they’d been gone, but when they got home, they rushed inside, drank water, and shook off the sand. Their parents saw the open gate and quickly closed it, saying, 'What good dogs we have—they didn’t run away!' Bravo and Buster barked happily and curled up in their cozy beds, tired from their adventure at New Smyrna Beach.

THE END

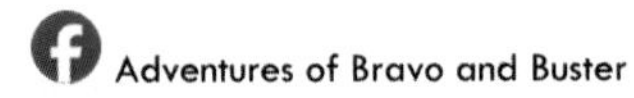
Adventures of Bravo and Buster

BookBaby
7905 Crescent Blvd. Pennsauken, NJ 088110
www.bookbaby.com 1-800 961-6878
Printed in the United States of America

Ordering Information:
Bookbaby.com, Amazon or Bethjjmj@gmail.com

Print ISBN: 979-8-35097-198-9

First Edition